Praise for *The Teensy Weensy V*

MW01139862

"A timely and developmentally appropriate aid for parents and grandparents to help their yo...
lives, and hopefully reduce the anxiety and emotional impact of the epidemic."

—William T. Burke, PhD, clinical psychologist
with forty years of clinical experience with children, adults, and families

"In simple, direct language that respects their ages, this story teaches preschoolers how to protect themselves and others against COVID-19. Its upbeat narrative and delightful illustrations will help young children understand the safety tips and precautions needed for their well-being during this pandemic. The accompanying song, 'The Teensy Weensy Virus,' is a fun bonus for readers."

—Barbara H. Dunn, PhD, RN, PNP of more than forty years,
clinician, consultant, author, mentor, and former faculty member at VCU and UVA Schools of Nursing,
Richmond, Virginia

"A soothing story that helps children understand the new world of COVID-19. It provides them with simple, proven steps for taking appropriate precautions, and will ease the anxiety that has accompanied this pandemic. An added benefit is the resource list provided for parents to learn more facts about this new disease."

—Helen Ragazzi, MD, FAAP
with twenty-four years of experience as a pediatrician

"Sherri Rose uses her characteristic straightforward sensitivity and undying optimism to make the unfathomable fathomable to both old and young. A developmentally appropriate, compassionate, and relatable mark of the times that is sure to be a hit with all generations as we struggle to make sense of the world around us."

—Kathryn King, MD, MHS
Associate Executive Medical Director at the Center for Telehealth,
Medical University of South Carolina

"I have two grandsons, three and five years old, and have already pictured reading this to them. This book takes a scary subject and provided beautiful, concrete, age-appropriate messaging about safety measures, protection, and love, all wrapped up in kid-friendly bubbles!"

—Carla Nye, DNP, CPNP-BC, CNE, CHSE
associate clinical professor and master's program director,
Department of Family and Community Health Nursing,
VCU School of Nursing, Richmond, VA

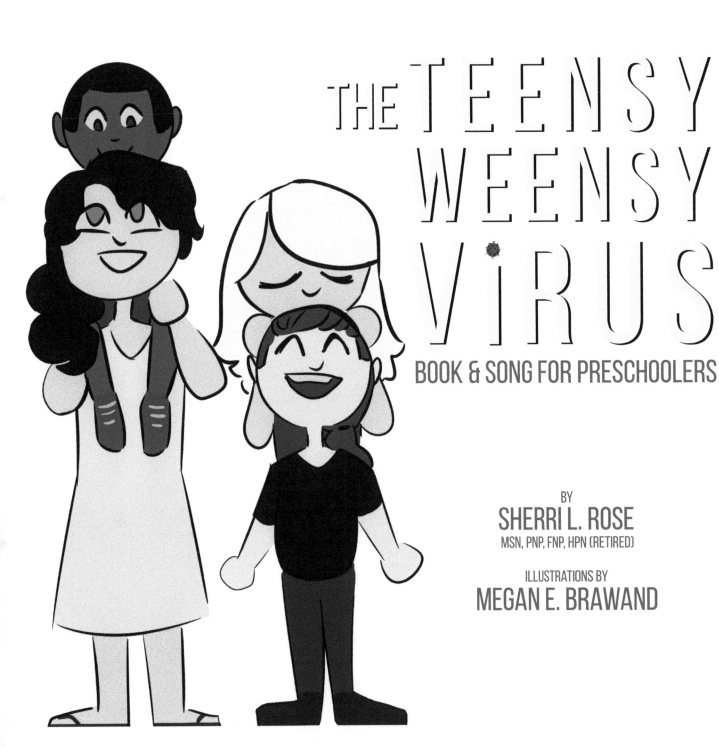

THE TEENSY WEENSY VIRUS

BOOK & SONG FOR PRESCHOOLERS

BY
SHERRI L. ROSE
MSN, PNP, FNP, HPN (RETIRED)

ILLUSTRATIONS BY
MEGAN E. BRAWAND

ISBN: 978-1-954003-00-2
LCCN: 2020923065

Printed in the United States of America

Dedicated to my precious youngest grandson,

Liam Odell Hall

whom I have not been able to hug since
March 10, 2020 due to COVID-19.

And to my older grandchildren:
Ryan, Ben, Erica, Megan, Lillian, and Thomas

Love, Sherri – "Mama Ri"

There can be no keener revelation of a society's soul

than the way in which it treats its children.

—Nelson Mandela

Introduction for Parents, Grandparents, and Caretakers

On March 11, 2020, the World Health Organization (WHO) declared that our world was in the throes of a global pandemic caused by the novel coronavirus, SARS-CoV-2. No healthcare practitioner or hospital was prepared for what was to come.

It took us all a while to better understand this brand-new virus and how it affects humans—young and old. It took some time to determine how it is spread, and what we can do to prevent contracting this very frightening virus. Long-term illnesses, hospitalizations, and deaths due to the virus have impacted us for months. We have now realized that asymptomatic people (people with no symptoms) can spread the virus to others—and that is indeed a pretty overwhelming fact.

Research into this virus is extensive and ongoing. As a retired nurse practitioner, I have the utmost respect for the government agencies that collect statistics and health data, work toward treatments and vaccines, and care for the people of the United States of America. The level of education of these physicians, researchers, and epidemiologists is remarkable, and critical in our fight against this virus. We must listen to them.

Please keep your families and children safe during this time.

Sherri L. Rose, MSN, PNP, FNP, HPN (Retired)

All of these recommendations, as well as the text of the book itself, have been written based on the author's best clinical interpretation of the scientific data available at the time of writing. Additional resources can be found at the end of this book.

One day, a teensy-weensy virus came along.

It was so teensy-weensy,

it was smaller than this dot!

•

People could catch this

teensy-weensy virus very easily.

And it made some people

really, really sick!

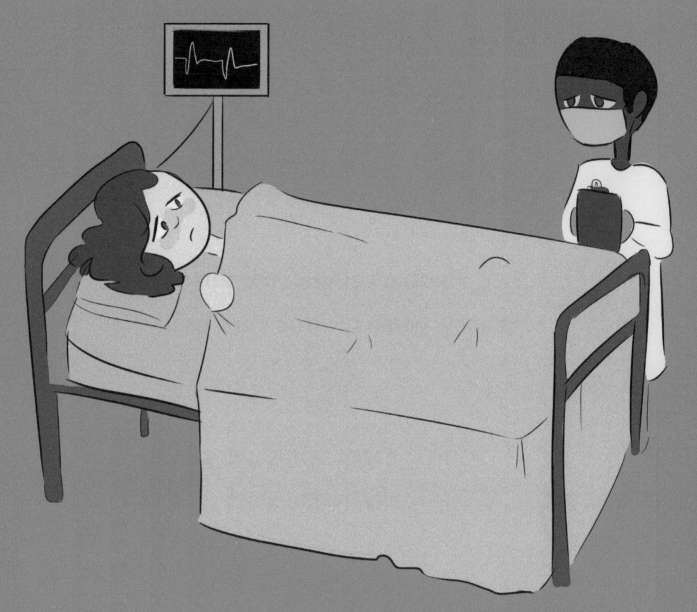

Some of those people got so sick,
they had to go to the hospital.

Their friends and family missed them
very much while they were away.

Everyone had to listen and follow directions
to keep from getting sick.

People had to start
wearing masks
when they went out.

11

They also had to wash
their hands A LOT!

WASH
UP!

SOAP

12

They also had to stay far away from people they didn't live with.

It was like each house and family was in its own bubble.

And when people went out,
their bubble went with them.

Sometimes it was easier for people to stay home,

so they would not catch the virus and get sick.

This made people sad

Because they could not visit some of their friends and family.

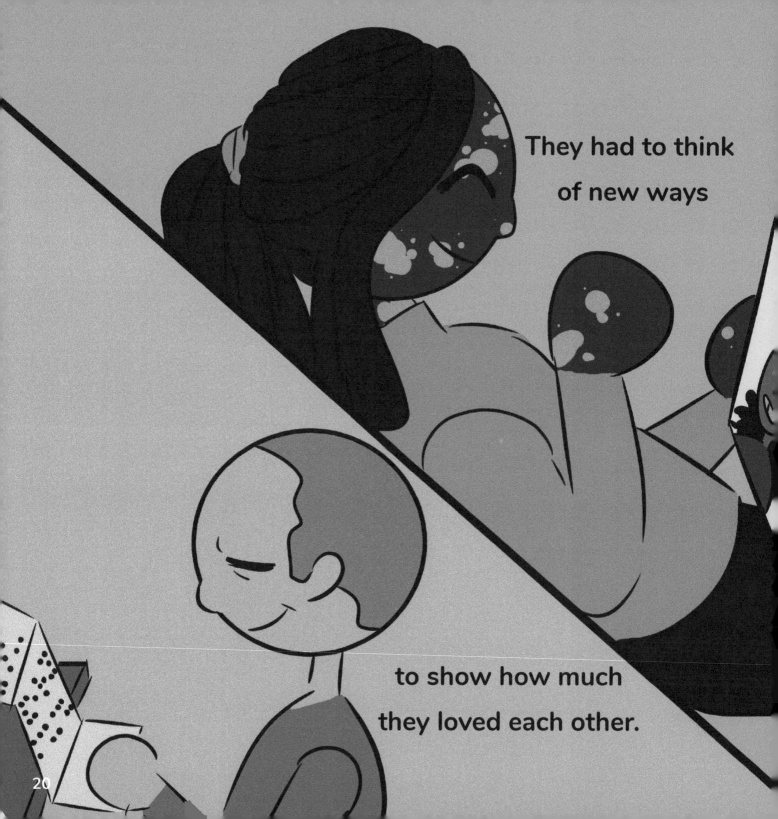

They had to think
of new ways

to show how much
they loved each other.

One day, this teensy-weensy virus
will not be so scary!

And we will be able to
visit our family and friends

And play together

And hug

each other

24

And see our grandmas or grandpas
or aunts or uncles or other people we love.

But until then . . .

It is important that we

wear our masks when we go out

Wash our hands (a lot!)

And listen to doctors
and scientists

Because . . .

We all love each other!

"The Teensy Weensy Virus"
(Sung to the tune of "The Itsy Bitsy Spider")

The Teensy Weensy Virus came along one day.

It makes people sick, so we have to stay away.

We wash our hands and wear our mask

When we go out to play,

So the Teensy Weensy Virus

Will finally go away!

The Teensy Weensy Virus

Sherri L. Rose

Traditional
arr. Evan Gregory

Additional Resources

1. For updates on the coronavirus around the world, visit the website of the World Health Organization (WHO): https://www.who.int/

2. For updates on the coronavirus within the United States, visit the website for the Centers for Disease Control and Prevention (CDC): https://www.cdc.gov/

3. For updates in your area, visit the websites of your state and local health departments. To find these, Google the name of your state, city, or county, followed by the phrase "health department." Their website should end in ".gov".

4. For information on how the coronavirus can affect our precious children, visit the website of the American Academy of Pediatrics (AAP): https://www.aap.org/. Most critically, the AAP has a special website for parents, https://www.healthychildren.org/, which is also available in Spanish.

5. For personal advice and recommendations for your and your child's physical health, listen to your doctor, to your child's pediatrician (especially if they are a Fellow in the American Academy of Pediatrics), and to nurse practitioners. Keeping families healthy is their priority, so please trust these and other healthcare workers.

6. Finally, for support for mental health issues, allow yourself to recognize that this has been a very traumatic period. The adjustments we have had to make to our lives to avoid catching the coronavirus have been so drastic, they can at times feel overwhelming.

During this time, it is more important than ever to protect your family's mental health. This virus has taken a significant emotional toll on all of us—adults, children, and families alike. But for some, this toll has been even worse than it has for others.

If you or your family have been affected by a death, disability, unemployment, or other hardship as a result of the coronavirus, seek support for your mental well-being. You can find resources in your local area through the following national agencies: the National Alliance on Mental Illness (https://www.nami.org) and Mental Health America (https://www.mhanational.org). Alternatively, seek assistance at your local department of social services or mental health services.

Taking steps to secure your mental well-being can be vital to the health of your child and your entire family. Don't hesitate to get help!

SHERRI ROSE grew up in Richmond, Virginia. As a retired pediatric and family nurse practitioner, as well as a hospice and palliative care nurse, she recognizes the critical importance of helping children understand what is happening during the pandemic that is currently sweeping the globe. COVID-19 has created so much stress, anxiety, grief, and loss for adults—imagine what children must think, but be unable to express!

Inspired by her concerns for the smallest among us—as well as by her own significant grief over not being able to hug her grandchildren during quarantine—Sherri began to write this book to help preschoolers understand what's going on and why all of us have to follow new rules. As a mother of three daughters and three stepdaughters, as well as a grandmother to many more, she hopes that the resources found in this book will be useful to parents and caregivers all over the world.

You can find more about Sherri on her website, www.sherrirosebooks.com.

MEGAN E. BRAWAND is a fifteen-year-old sophomore at Thomas Dale High School in Chester, Virginia. She loves to draw, paint, and create digital artwork as a way of combining her thoughts and feelings. Her artwork has been included at several local art exhibits, and in 2018, at age thirteen, she created a painting that was chosen for display at Crossroads Art Center in Richmond, Virginia.

Megan's other interests include theatre production, sci-fi themes, and vintage automobiles. She plans to attend college to pursue a career in concept art so she may create illustrations that convey a writer's ideas prior to production. Megan is humbled and honored to collaborate with this author on such a wonderful book!

The members of the Gregory Brothers: Michael, Andrew, Evan, and Sarah Fullen Gregory.

Sherri wrote the lyrics for "The Teensy Weensy Virus" with a little help from THE GREGORY BROTHERS, a Brooklyn-based quartet specializing in comedy music. They also arranged the musical score, which can be purchased at www.sherrirosebooks.com/about-the-song. The arrangement makes for a great song for string players and new pianists.

In addition to their work on "The Teensy Weensy Virus," the Gregory Brothers are the creators of the video series Auto-Tune the News and Songify This. You can watch their videos, which have been viewed over one billion times, at www.youtube.com/songify.

CPSIA information can be obtained
at www.ICGtesting.com
Printed in the USA
BVHW021758191220
596066BV00003B/52